GET INTO KNITTING

GET-INTO-IT
GUIDES

JANICE DYER

CRABTREE
Publishing Company
www.crabtreebooks.com

Author: Janice Dyer

Editors:
Marcia Abramson, Philip Gebhardt, Janine Deschenes

Photo research: Melissa McClellan

Editorial director: Kathy Middleton

Proofreader: Wendy Scavuzzo

Cover/Interior Design: T.J. Choleva

**Production coordinator and
   Prepress technician:** Samara Parent

Print coordinator: Katherine Berti

Consultant: Margaret Amy Salter – Co-host of international knitting podcast Knit 1 Geek 2

Knitting Project Designer
All knitting projects in this book created by Sarah Hodgson

Developed and produced for Crabtree Publishing by BlueApple*Works* Inc.

Photographs

Shutterstock.com: © Melica (2cd from top left inset); © se media (cover boy top); © Stone36 (cover boy bottom); © Salman Timur (cover background); © Claudia Carlsen (TOC); © Picsfive (TOC bottom); © Viktor Kunz (p. 4 right); © Kzenon (p. 6 top left); © Teresa Levite (p. 6 top right); © : Fleckstone (p. 6 2cd from top right); © revers (p. 6 2cd from bottom right); © shooarts (p. 6 bottom right); © Jiggo_thekop (p. 7 top left); © SneSivan (p. 7 top middle); © Oliver Hoffmann (p. 7 top right); © stockphoto mania (p. 7 middle right); © Eric Isselee (p. 7 middle right); © vladis.studio (Knit Bit); © Sarah Marchant (p. 13 top left, p. 13 top right); © Tetiana Dziubanovska (p. 13 top middle); © Robynrg (p. 22 bottom left, cover inset); © azure1 (p. 23 bottom right); © Beskova Ekaterina (handmade label); © oliveromg (p. 29 bottom left);

Thinkstock: Jupiterimages (title page);

© Austen Photography (cover insets, p. 8, 9, 10, 11, 12, 13 bottom right, 14, 15, 16, 17, 18, 19, 20, 22, 23, 24, 25, 26, 27, 28);

© Sam Taylor (cover girl, p. 4 left, 5 bottom right, 7 bottom, 8 bottom right, 13 bottom left, 18 bottom right, 19 bottom right, 20 top left, 20 bottom right, 25 bottom right, 27 bottom right, 28 bottom right, 30, 31, backcover);

Creative Commons: Baykedevries (p. 5 top left); Shrewdcat (p. 5 top right);

Public Domain: Newland 2 (p. 29 top right)

Library and Archives Canada Cataloguing in Publication

Dyer, Janice, author
      Get into knitting / Janice Dyer.

(Get-into-it guides)
Includes index.
Issued also in print and electronic formats.
ISBN 978-0-7787-2641-8 (hardback).--ISBN 978-0-7787-2647-0 (paperback).--ISBN 978-1-4271-1792-2 (html)

      1. Knitting--Juvenile literature. I. Title.

TT820 D94 2016   j746.43'2   C2016-903391-0
                                                      C2016-903392-9

Library of Congress Cataloging-in-Publication Data

Names: Dyer, Janice, author.
Title: Get into knitting / Janice Dyer.
Description: New York, New York : Crabtree Publishing Company, [2017] | Series: Get-into-it guides | Audience: Ages 8-11. | Audience: Grades 4-6. | Includes index.
Identifiers: LCCN 2016029170 (print) | LCCN 2016031892 (ebook) | ISBN 9780778726418 (reinforced library binding : alk. paper) | ISBN 9780778726470 (pbk. : alk. paper) | ISBN 9781427117922 (Electronic HTML)
Subjects: LCSH: Knitting--Juvenile literature.
Classification: LCC TT820 .D94 2017 (print) | LCC TT820 (ebook) | DDC 746.43/2--dc23
LC record available at https://lccn.loc.gov/2016029170

Crabtree Publishing Company

www.crabtreebooks.com   1-800-387-7650

Printed in Canada/072016/EF20160630

**Published in Canada
Crabtree Publishing**
616 Welland Ave.
St. Catharines, Ontario
L2M 5V6

**Published in the United States
Crabtree Publishing**
PMB 59051
350 Fifth Avenue, 59th Floor
New York, New York 10118

**Published in the United Kingdom
Crabtree Publishing**
Maritime House
Basin Road North, Hove
BN41 1WR

**Published in Australia
Crabtree Publishing**
3 Charles Street
Coburg North
VIC, 3058

CONTENTS

WHAT IS KNITTING?

Knitting is a fun activity for everyone! When you knit, you create and interlock many loops of **yarn**, called stitches. The stitches form rows on special needles. The more rows you add, the longer the result.

You can use different kinds of stitches to create different **textures** and looks for the final product. There are also many different types of yarn and needle sizes. You can make clothing, accessories, and other items from knitting.

Knitting is a great way to relax. You can knit while watching TV or chatting with your friends. Many places have knitting clubs where people get together in groups to learn how to knit and to meet other knitters. Maybe you could join or start a knitting club at your school!

Yarn comes in many colors, textures, and thicknesses.

4

The History of Knitting

Many believe that knitting started with ancient people using knots to create fishing nets. But it is hard to figure out exactly when knitting first began because the yarn used for knitting breaks down and **decomposes** very quickly. The oldest piece of knitting was a pair of cotton socks discovered in Egypt. Experts believe that the socks are from 300–499 c.e. They are on display in a museum in London, England.

Most of the early pieces of knitting were made from cotton or silk. These materials were easy to get in the Middle East, where many believe knitting began. Paintings from the 14th century show that knitting became more popular in Europe around that time.

Knit Bit

Yarn bombing or graffiti knitting is a type of street art created by mystery knitters. Knitters cover large objects such as trees, statues, lampposts, bicycles, and even buses with colorful yarn to create art!

How to Use This Book

Start by learning the stitches, then try the projects. Each project tells you what size needles to use and how much yarn you need. Knitting is a skill that requires a lot of practice. Master these projects, and you will be well on your way to being a knitter! Many of the projects would make great gifts, so you can make more than one of each and get even more practice. The more you knit, the better you will get at it.

You can knit anywhere! All you need to get started is a pair of needles and a ball of yarn.

5

TOOLS AND MATERIALS

You can buy yarn and the tools you need for knitting at yarn shops, sewing and craft stores, and department stores. Many yarn shops also offer free help to knitters.

*Yarn weight refers to the thickness of yarn. Changing yarn weight or needle size makes a big difference to the finished project, so **standardized** systems have been created.*

YARN

Yarn comes in many different shapes and sizes. The type of yarn you choose to use will depend on the project you are working on.

Yarn also comes in different thicknesses. If you are knitting baby clothes or blankets, you will want to use very **fine yarn** that is soft to the touch. Thicker yarn is good for blankets and sweaters, while **bulky yarn** is perfect for scarves and rugs.

Yarn can be made from a variety of natural **fibers**, such as wool and silk, cotton, and linen. Synthetics are human-made fibers and are also known as acrylic fibers. Acrylic yarns are lightweight, soft, and warm, and feel like wool.

Knit Bit

Worsted weight yarn (medium weight) is named for the village of Worstead, England. Worstead was a center for manufacturing fiber, both yarn and cloth, in the 12th century.

YARN PACKAGES

- A hank is a long loop of yarn twisted into a bundle.
- A skein is an oblong-shaped ball of yarn. A skein is ready-to-use, and no winding is necessary.
- A ball is the round shape that results from hand-winding yarn.
- A cake is a cylinder with a flat top and bottom that comes off a ball winder. A ball winder is a small machine that changes hanks of yarn into cakes.

Hank

Skein

Ball

Cake

KNITTING NEEDLES

Knitting needles come in different diameters and lengths. They can be made of bamboo or other wood, plastic, steel, or aluminum. The type of project you are working on will determine what size of needle to choose. For example, the thicker the needle, the larger the stitches you will make. The result will be a loose **fabric**. Smaller needles will create tighter fabric. If you are making a small project, you might want to use shorter needles.

The most common needles used are straight needles. They have one pointed end and a knob on the other end to stop the stitches from falling off.

WOOL

Wool comes from many different types of animals, including sheep, goats, llamas, alpacas, camels, rabbits, muskox, and opossums. In fact, yarn can be made from the fur or hair of any animal. People have even knit with the fur that their pet cats and dogs have shed!

*Cashmere wool comes from goats and is very **luxurious** and soft. It takes the hair of more than two goats to make one sweater.*

One sheep can provide enough wool for many sweaters.

Alpaca wool is soft and warm.

WIND A BALL FROM A HANK

Some yarn that you buy comes in a coil called a hank. If you knit using the hank, your yarn will become tangled, so you need to wind the hank into a ball.

First, find the end of the yarn. Lightly wrap the yarn around your fingers. Remove the wrapped loops and keep wrapping the yarn around the loops.

Change directions every 15 to 20 rounds. Continue until you have a round ball of yarn.

CASTING ON

Once you have all your tools and materials, you are ready to start knitting! First you make a slip knot to attach the yarn to the needle. Then you cast on, which means putting a row of stitches on your needle.

SLIP KNOT FOR THE FIRST STITCH

1 *Make a loop with the end of your yarn. Make sure the yarn crosses over itself.*

2 *Make another loop and pull it through the first loop.*

3 *Make the new loop big enough to fit over your needle.*

The loose end that is left is called the tail.

4 *Put the needle through the loop.*

5 *Pull the yarn to make the knot. It should be snug, but not too tight. It should be able to slip along the needle.*

KNIT TIP
The slip knot counts as the first stitch.

Now you need to cast on, which means adding stitches to your needle. The more stitches you cast on, the wider your knitted piece will be. The first row is basically a series of loops. A **knitting pattern** will always tell you how many loops to make. Count them to make sure you have the same number of loops as the pattern asks for.

KNIT TIP

Practice casting on before you start a project. Fill a row of stitches and then pull them off and do it again. After a bit of practice, it will be easy!

1 2 3 4 5 6 7 8 9 10

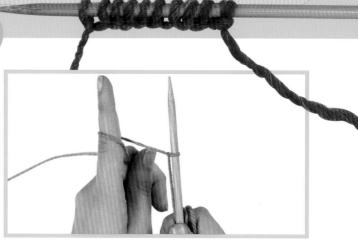

LOOP CAST ON

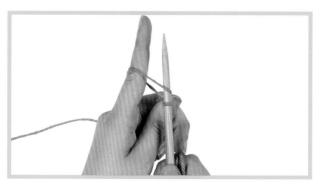

1 *Hold the needle with the slip knot in your right hand. Hold the yarn attached to the yarn ball with your left hand.*

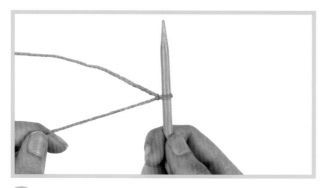

2 *Wrap the yarn in your left hand around your finger from right to left, making a loop.*

HOLDING NEEDLES

Different cultures have their own styles of holding knitting needles. Individual people develop their own styles, too. There is no one right way. If your knitting looks good and you feel comfortable, you have found the right style for you.

3 *Put the needle underneath the yarn looped over your finger. Pull your finger out from the yarn, leaving the loop on the needle.*

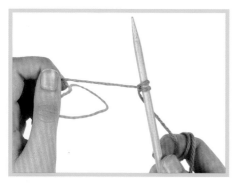

4 *Pull the loop on your knitting needle tight—you have made a stitch! Make sure the yarn is snug, but not too tight.*

5 *Repeat these steps until you have cast on 10 stitches.*

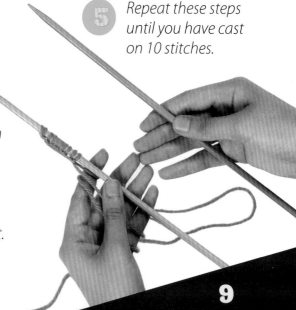

KNIT STITCH

Once you have cast on 10 stitches, you are ready to start knitting! This basic stitch is called the knit stitch. These instructions work for right-handed people.

1 Hold the needle with the cast-on stitches in your left hand, and the empty needle in your right hand. Slide the right-hand needle into the first stitch on the left-hand needle, and push it behind the needle.

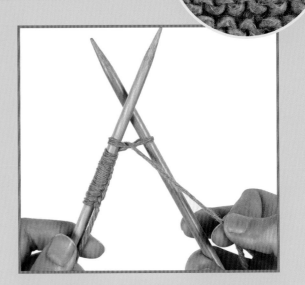

2 Loop the yarn attached to the ball **counterclockwise** over the point of the right-hand needle, and pull the yarn down between the two needles. Don't pull too tightly!

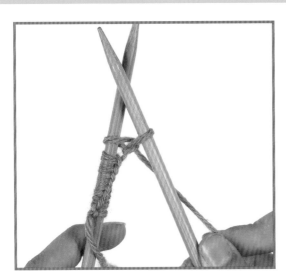

3 Dip the point of the right-hand needle down into the top stitch. Bring the point of the needle forward, taking only the wrapped yarn with it.

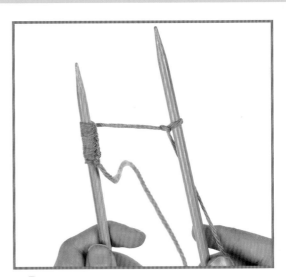

4 Slowly lift the stitch up and off of the left-hand needle. The new loop is on the right-hand needle, and the tail is still on the left-hand needle.

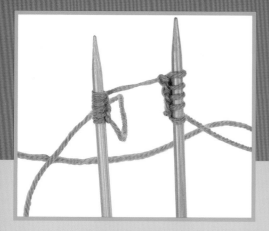

5 Repeat the knit stitch until you have knit every stitch on the left-hand needle, and they are all on the right-hand needle. This is your first row of knitting!

Knit Bit

Garter stitch is a pattern created when every row is done in knit stitch.

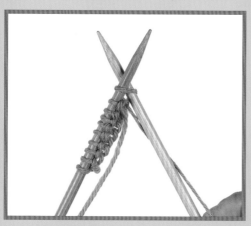

6 Switch needles. All the finished stitches should be on the needle in your left hand, and the empty needle should be in your right hand. Start on your second row. Knit every row and keep switching needles. Watch as your knitting grows!

OOPS!

Your knitting looks like an open weave. This means your knitting is too loose. Try wrapping the yarn around the needles a bit tighter.

Knit Tip

Make sure your stitches don't get too tight. You will know your knitting is tight if you have trouble getting your needles into the stitches. One way to keep your knitting loose is to make sure you don't knit at the very tip of the knitting needles. Each stitch should be on the fat part of the needle before you begin your next stitch. Another way is to relax your hands when you are holding your needles. Don't grip or pull the yarn too hard.

Rows

Counting Rows

A row of knitting is made up of all the stitches on a needle. As you knit, you create rows of knitting stacked on top of each other. When you are counting rows of knitting, you are counting the number of rows in the stack.

PURL STITCH

Now that you have mastered the knit stitch, it's time to learn the purl stitch. Using the knit stitch and purl stitch together will make your project look amazing!

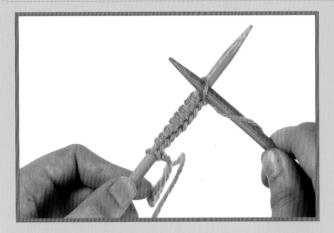

1. Hold the needle with the cast-on stitches in your left hand and the empty needle in your right hand. Slide the right-hand needle into the first stitch on the left-hand needle in front of the left-hand needle.

2. Loop the yarn attached to the ball counterclockwise over the point of the right-hand needle. Don't pull too tightly!

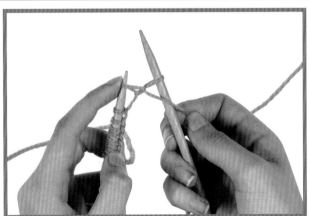

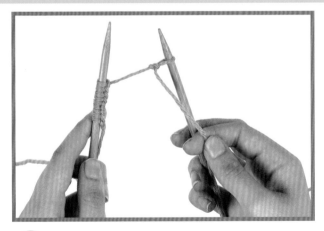

3. Tilt the right-hand needle back up through the stitch on the left-hand needle, taking only the wrapped yarn with it.

4. Lift the new loop off. Make sure to keep the new loop on the right-hand needle and the tail on the left-hand needle. Repeat until all the finished stitches are on the needle in your right hand. Switch needles and purl another row.

KNIT TIP

Check out the recommended video lesson to see exactly how this is done. Find the Web link on page 30.

STOCKINETTE STITCH

The stockinette stitch, or stocking stitch, is one of the easiest knitting stitches and is great for beginners. You can see the stockinette stitch in many different kinds of knitting projects, such as scarves, socks, sweaters, hats, blankets, and much more. The front side of the fabric is smooth, and the stitches look like small v's. The back side looks like bumpy ridges. To knit this stitch, you alternate a row of knit stitches with a row of purl stitches.

Follow these steps to knit the stockinette stitch:

■ Row 1: Knit   ■ Row 2: Purl   ■ Repeat these 2 rows.

It's as easy as that!

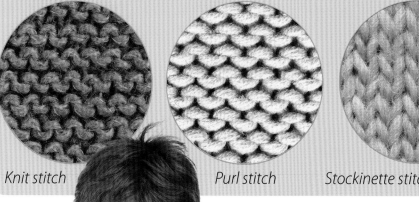

Knit stitch   *Purl stitch*   *Stockinette stitch (knit one row, purl one row)*

KNITTING STRIPES

Using a lot of color in your knitting is fun and makes your finished project more interesting. You can make narrow stripes or wide stripes, and you can use any stitch. It is also a great way to use up leftover yarn. Try making a striped scarf with many colors!

HOW TO KNIT STRIPES

Knitting stripes isn't hard. You just need to join one color of yarn to the next. Change colors at the end of a row so that the rows stay even.

1 *Cut the yarn of the original color, leaving 10 inches (25 cm) of tail. Make a slip knot with the new color. Pass the original color yarn through it.*

2 *Slip the knot up to the needle.*

3 *Begin knitting with the new color.*

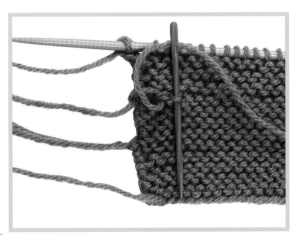

4 *Keep knitting with the new color until you want to make another stripe, then repeat steps 1 through 3. **Darn** in all the loose ends as you go, or when you are finished (see page 17).*

DECREASING

If you want to knit more than just a square or rectangle, you need to be able to decrease while knitting. This means you reduce the number of stitches on the needle. By decreasing the number of stitches, you can shape your final product.

HOW TO KNIT DECREASES

When you knit decreases, the knitted piece will get narrower as you work. The easiest way to knit decreases is to knit two stitches together.

1 *Slide your needle under the first and second stitch.*

2 *Knit the two stitches together as if they were one stitch. Pull the stitch off the needle. You are treating two stitches like one. Knit the rest of the stitches normally. Count the stitches and now there is one less.*

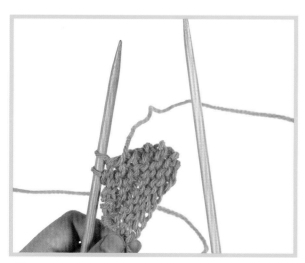

3 *If you keep decreasing, each row will have fewer stitches.*

OOPS!

There are holes in your project. This means you have added an extra stitch. Count your stitches every few rows to make sure you have the same number of stitches as you cast on.

CASTING OFF

After you have finished your knitting project, you need to **cast off** the stitches of the last row to make an even edge that won't unravel. Here is how to cast off.

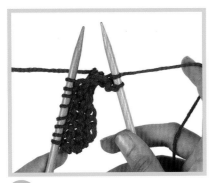

1 Knit the first two stitches from the left-hand needle onto the right-hand needle.

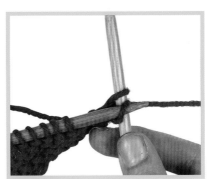

2 Push the tip of the left-hand needle into the first stitch on the right-hand needle.

3 Lift the first stitch over the second stitch and drop it off the right-hand needle. Knit another stitch from the left-hand needle onto the right-hand needle and do the same again. Continue this process with each stitch until there is only one stitch on the right-hand needle.

OOPS!

You made a mistake. Don't worry, every knitter makes them. Pulling out stitches gives you more practice, and more practice makes you a better knitter.

4 Cut the yarn, leaving a 6-inch (15 cm) end. Pull out the needle.

5 Gently pull on the last stitch to make it a bit bigger. Pull the end of the yarn through the loop.

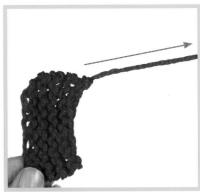

6 Pull the yarn tight.

SEWING TECHNIQUES

When you are finished a piece, you need to darn the loose ends. Sometimes you also need to sew pieces together to create a final product, or you might want to add a button or two. Here are some techniques to use.

Darning In Loose Ends

*At the end of a knitting project, you need to weave in the ends of the yarn that are hanging from the project. Weaving in the ends makes your project look neat and finished, and keeps the ends from getting loose. To darn in the ends, **thread** a **yarn needle** with the end of the yarn and work the yarn through some stitches on the wrong side of the project.*

Sew Together

Poke the yarn needle up through the green fabric from the back to the front, then down through the orange fabric about ¼ inch (0.5 cm) to the left. Pull the yarn gently to tighten it, but not so tight that the fabric puckers. Keep poking the needle up then down through the fabrics in ¼ inch (0.5 cm) intervals, gently pulling the yarn tight.

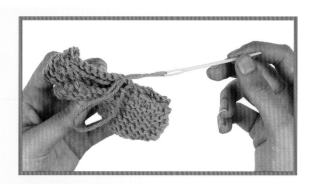

Sew On a Button

Cut a short piece of yarn about 6 inches (15 cm). Tie a knot at one end. Thread the other end through a yarn needle. Hold the button in place on the right side of the piece and bring the needle from the wrong side, or back of the fabric, through one of the holes in the button. Take the needle back through another hole. If there are four holes, make an X. Remove the yarn from the needle and tie a knot at the back. Trim the ends.

Knit Tip

When threading a yarn needle, fold the yarn over and insert the loop through the hole.

SCARF PROJECT

A scarf is an easy project to start with. You cast on and you knit. Then you cast off. That's it. It is a great way to practice and work on getting your stitches nice and even.

YOU WILL NEED

- Worsted weight wool (2 balls)
- US 15 (10 mm) knitting needles

VARIEGATED YARN

Variegated yarn is a yarn that has been dyed with more than one color. It can produce different patterns, including stripes. Both the cowl and scarf on these pages were made with variegated yarn.

1 Cast on 20 stitches.

2 Knit each row until you reach 28 inches (71 cm) or your desired length.

3 Cast off. Darn in the loose ends.

18

Easy Tassels

You can add tassels to the ends of your scarf. Make them in the same color or different colors.

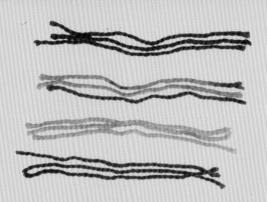

You Will Need

- *Worsted weight wool (less than 1 ball)*
- *Crochet hook*

1 Cut several lengths of yarn (about 6 inches (15 cm) for each tassel.

2 Fold three pieces of yarn in half. Starting with the bottom corner of one end of the scarf, use the **crochet hook** to pull the strand through.

3 Pull the loop partway through. Pull the ends of the yarn through the loop and pull tight.

4 Make more tassels along the bottom edges. Leave space in-between. When finished, check that all the tassels are the same length and trim any that are too long.

Scarf Variation: Make a Cowl

A cowl is a scarf with the ends sewn together. Sometimes a cowl is long enough to go around your neck once, and sometimes it is longer and goes around a few times.

Materials and Instructions

- *Super bulky weight yarn (1 ball)*
- *US 15 (10 mm) knitting needles*

1. *Cast on 15 stitches.*
2. *Knit until the cowl fits loosely around your neck. Cast off. Darn in loose ends.*
3. *Using a yarn needle, sew together the two ends.*

PILLOW PROJECT

Knitting with bulky thick yarn is fun. The yarn is so thick that you will easily see mistakes so you can quickly fix them. Use it to make a pillow to decorate your room.

You Will Need

- ■ *Bulky fun yarn (1 ball color A, 1 ball color B) or super bulky yarn (2 balls)*
- ■ *US 15 (10 mm) knitting needles*
- ■ *Yarn needle*
- ■ *Craft stuffing*

1 *Cast on 20 stitches in color A of bulky fun yarn, or cast on 15 stitches in super bulky yarn.*

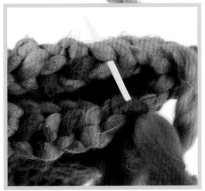

2 *Knit in stockinette stitch (1 row knit, 1 row purl) for 12 inches (30 cm). Cast off. Darn in loose ends.*

3 *Repeat steps 1 and 2 with the other color of yarn if you are doing a two-color pillow, or with the same yarn for a matching color.*

4 *Using a yarn needle, sew together three sides.*

oops!

You have run out of yarn. Join a new ball using the same technique as when knitting stripes (page 14).

Knit Tip

Knitting grows fast when you use bulky yarn. It is also easy to see how you are doing! Use this yarn for big projects such as pillows and scarves.

Cell Phone Sock

A cell phone sock is a great way to cover and protect your cell phone. Here's how to knit a colorful cell phone sock.

Materials and Instructions

- *Worsted weight wool (1 ball)*
- *US 6 (4 mm) knitting needles*
- *Yarn needle*

1. *Cast on 15 stitches.*
2. *Knit in stockinette stitch (1 row knit, 1 row purl).*
3. *Continue until the piece measures twice the length of your phone.*
4. *Cast off. Darn in the loose ends.*
5. *Fold in half. Using a yarn needle, sew together each long side, leaving an opening at the top.*

5 *Stuff with craft stuffing.*

6 *Use a yarn needle to sew together the last side/opening.*

DOG COLLAR PROJECT

You can make a decorative collar for your dog using **reflective yarn**. Reflective yarn includes special threads that reflect light, even after it has been washed. This makes the yarn easy to see at night. Use Velcro to attach the knitted collar to your dog's regular collar for safety.

You Will Need

- Bulky yarn (1 ball)
- US 8 (5 mm) knitting needles
- Button(s)
- Yarn needle
- Measuring tape
- Glue
- Velcro
- Sewing needle & thread

1. Depending on the size of your dog, cast on stitches:
   Small – Cast on 4 stitches
   Medium – Cast on 6 stitches
   Large – Cast on 8 stitches
   Extra-large – Cast on 10 stitches

2. Measure your dog's collar with a measuring tape. Knit each row until the collar is the length you measured. Cast off. Darn in loose ends.

3. Bring the ends of the collar together to make a circle, overlapping about ½ inch (1.3 cm). Use a yarn needle to sew the ends together.

4. Decorate by sewing on a fancy button or two.

5. Glue one part of a Velcro strip to your dog's collar. Sew the other part to the knit collar. Join the two Velcro parts.

TOY COLLAR PROJECT

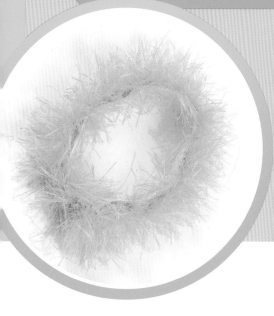

You can make a decorative collar for your stuffed animals using eyelash yarn, which is a **novelty yarn**. This type of yarn has strands of fiber coming off of it that look like eyelashes—and it's soft and fuzzy!

Note: This project is for stuffed toys only. Eyelash yarn is not safe for real-life pets.

YOU WILL NEED

- *Eyelash yarn (1 ball)*
- *US 4 (3.5 mm) knitting needles*
- *Thread*
- *Sewing elastic*
- *Sewing needle*

1. *Measure a thin piece of sewing elastic around your stuffed toy's neck, keeping it a little loose. Make a mark, then cut the elastic.*

2. *Cast on 4 stitches. Knit each row until the length is 1 inch (2.5 cm) longer than the piece of elastic.*

3. *Cast off. Darn in loose ends.*

4. *Pin the elastic to the collar using safety pins.*

5. *Sew the elastic to the knit collar using a yarn needle and the same yarn. Sew all ends together.*

STUFFED OWL PROJECT

Learn how to knit stripes while making a cute stuffed owl—or two or three!

YOU WILL NEED

- *Worsted weight yarn (1 ball each color)*
- *US 7 (4.5 mm) knitting needles*
- *Buttons*
- *Yarn needle*
- *Craft stuffing*

1 *Cast on 18 stitches in color A. Knit each row until you have knit 3 inches (7.5 cm).*

2 *With the right side facing away from you, change to color B. Knit each row until you have 4 inches (10 cm) of color B.*

3 *With the right side facing away from you, change back to color A. Knit each row until you have knit 3 inches (7.5 cm). You will have knit a total of 10 inches (25 cm). Cast off.*

4 *Use a yarn needle to darn in the loose ends. Fold the knitted piece in half, right sides together, and use a yarn needle to sew each side together. Leave the bottom open for stuffing. Turn right side out.*

5 *Using a yarn needle and yarn, sew on buttons for the eyes.*

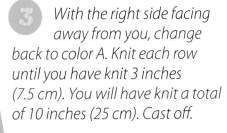

Mini Scarf for the Owl

You can add a mini scarf to your stuffed owl to finish the project.

Materials and Instructions

- *Worsted weight yarn*
- *US 7 (4.5 mm) knitting needles*
- *Yarn needle*

1. *Cast on 5 stitches.*
2. *Knit for 12 inches (30 cm).*
3. *Cast off.*
4. *Darn loose ends using a yarn needle.*
5. *Tie scarf around owl where the colors change.*

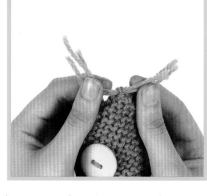

6 Cut several pieces of yarn about 2 inches (5 cm) each in length. Using a yarn needle, thread and tie several pieces of yarn to create ear tufts.

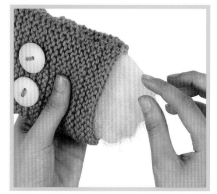

7 Stuff the owl with craft stuffing. Using a yarn needle, sew up the bottom.

HAT PROJECT

Practice knitting decreases while making a cool hat. Make one with stripes (see page 14), and add a pom-pom for decoration.

YOU WILL NEED

- Worsted weight yarn (1 ball or 1 each of two colors for stripes)
- US 7 (4.5 mm) knitting needles
- Yarn needle

KNIT TIP

To avoid tangles, pull the yarn from the center of a ball whenever possible, not from the outside.

1 Cast on 80 stitches.

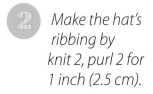

2 Make the hat's ribbing by knit 2, purl 2 for 1 inch (2.5 cm).

3 With the right side facing you, knit in stockinette stitch for 4 inches (10 cm).

4 Begin decreasing:

Row 1 — (Knit 6, knit 2 together) repeat across row
Row 2 — Purl
Row 3 — (Knit 5, knit 2 together) repeat across row
Row 4 — Purl
Row 5 — (Knit 4, knit 2 together) repeat across row
Row 6 — Purl
Row 7 — (Knit 3, knit 2 together) repeat across row
Row 8 — Purl
Row 9 — (Knit 2, knit 2 together) repeat across row
Row 10 — Purl
Row 11 — (Knit 1, knit 2 together) repeat across row
Row 12 — Purl
Row 13 — (Knit 2 together) repeat across row

YOU WILL NEED

■ Piece of cardboard 3 x 5 in (7.5 x 13 cm) ■ scissors ■ wool

1 Cut a rectangle out of a piece of cardboard. Start winding yarn around it. You can make it all one color of yarn or wind different colors together.

2 Continue winding until you have a thick band. The more you wind, the thicker the pom-pom. (It takes about 150 winds for a very thick pom-pom.) Cut the yarn from the ball. Bend the cardboard slightly to remove the yarn.

3 Cut a long piece of yarn. Center the band of yarn on top of it. Tie a very tight knot. Tie a couple more knots to secure it.

4 Cut all the loops, but don't cut the tie. Fluff the pom-pom with your fingers. Trim the ends to make it even.

5 To attach the pom-pom to the hat, place the ends of the yarn in the yarn needle. Pull through the top of the hat. Repeat several times. Turn the hat inside out. Tie the two ends together and trim.

5 Cut the yarn and weave through the remaining stitches.

6 Using a yarn needle, weave in the ends and sew the back seam.

DISH CLOTH PROJECT

You can learn how to knit a pattern while making dish cloths to use as gifts! It's good for the environment to reuse the same cloths over and over, too.

You Will Need

- Worsted weight cotton yarn (1 ball)
- US 6 (4 mm) knitting needles
- Yarn needle

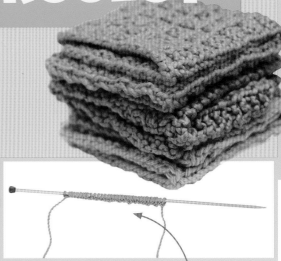

 2 Repeat the following 4-row pattern until your work measures 8½ inches (22 cm), ending with a row 4. If it measures the right length but you are not at row 4, keep knitting until you are.

Row 1— Knit
Row 2 — Knit 2, purl to last 2 stitches, knit 2
Row 3 — Knit 2, (knit 1, purl 2) x 11, knit 3
Row 4 — Knit 2, (purl 1, knit 2) x 12

1 Cast on 38 stitches.

Pattern Tip The line (knit 1, purl 2) x 11 means that everything in the brackets is to be repeated as many times as indicated by the number after x. In this case, it is 11 times.

3 Cast off and darn in loose ends.

4 Tie a ribbon around the cloth, or cloths if you make more than one. Attach your label if you decide to make one.

Knit Tip

Make labels to show your gift was handmade by you! Draw a label on a piece of card stock, then cut the label out. Punch a small hole at the top. Cut a small piece of yarn and thread it through the hole. Tie it to any gift you make.

EXTREME KNITTING!

Extreme knitting is knitting with giant needles and jumbo yarn or rope. Extreme knitters make throws, blankets, and pieces of art that can weigh up to 200 pounds (91 kg)!

The blankets made by extreme knitters are the largest, warmest, and fuzziest blankets you will ever see. The special wool used for extreme knitting is very thick and bulky. Some extreme knitters mix many strands of yarn together to create thicker yarn for their projects. There are also special patterns and oversized knitting needles you can buy if you want to try this extreme craft.

Julia Hopson set a world record using knitting needles that are 11½ feet (3.5 m) long.

CLOTHING AND ACCESSORIES

Extreme knitters create oversized clothing and chunky accessories with their jumbo yarn and giant needles. These projects are soft and bulky and have a gorgeous texture. It takes longer to do extreme knitting because the tools are so big to hold, but the unique results are well worth it. Some knitters even knit using their arms as needles!

You can use extreme knitting yarn to create a wrap or hat with added style.

BOOKS

Learn to knit 6 great projects (Klutz-book and kit) by Anne Akers Johnson. Klutz Press, 2013.

My First Knitting Book by Alison McNicol. Kyle Craig Publishing, 2012.

Knitting for Children: 35 Simple Knits Kids Will Love to Make by Claire Montgomerie. CICO Books, 2011.

WEBSITES

WIKI HOW to do anything
www.wikihow.com/Knit
Step-by-step instructions for learning how to knit. The site includes instructions for left-handers.

Painting Lilies
www.paintinglilies.com/knitting/ 2-free-beginner-knitting-patterns/
Links to free knitting patterns for beginners.

KNIT TIP – PURL STITCH ON PAGE 12
http://newstitchaday.com/ knitting-101-how-to-knit- the-purl-stitch-for-beginners/

Check out the recommended video lesson to see exactly how this is done.

GLOSSARY

bulky yarn Thick yarn

cast off To remove stitches from a knitting needle at the end of a project

counterclockwise In the opposite direction of the hands of a clock

crochet hook A tool with a small hook at the end

darn To sew with a row of stitches

decompose To slowly break down and decay

fabric Woven or knitted material

fiber A material made from thin threads used to form a yarn

fine yarn Thin yarn that is very soft to the touch

knitting pattern The written step-by-step instructions for creating a knitted item

luxurious Very comfortable and elegant

novelty yarn A different and unusual type of yarn

reflective yarn A special kind of yarn made with thread that reflects light

standardized Made consistent by developing rules

texture The way something feels or looks

thread To push thread or yarn through the eye of a needle for sewing

variegated With sections of different colors

yarn A long, thin piece of fiber used for knitting

yarn needle A large plastic or metal sewing needle

INDEX